PUFFINS

by Jaclyn Jaycox

PEBBLE
a capstone imprint

Pebble Explore is published by Pebble, an imprint of Capstone.
1710 Roe Crest Drive
North Mankato, Minnesota 56003
www.capstonepub.com

Library of Congress Cataloging-in-Publication data is available on the Library of Congress website.
ISBN 978-1-9771-2318-3 (library binding)
ISBN 978-1-9771-2652-8 (paperback)
ISBN 978-1-9771-2326-8 (eBook PDF)

Summary: Text describes puffins, including where they live, their bodies, what they do, and dangers to puffins.

Image Credits
Alamy: agefotostock, 1, Ann and Steve Toon, 28, Nature Picture Library, 14; Capstone Press, 6; Shutterstock: Anthony Smith Images, 1, 11, Blue Planet Studio, Cover, DWeeks, 25, gabrisigno, 21, Greg and Jan Ritchie, 22, Johann Ragnarsson, 27, Katkami, 10, Maksimilian, 23, Mark Cane, 13, Mark Medcalf, 18, Menno Schaefer, 26, Michael Zysman, 7, mikemaginn, 5, PJ photography, 9, Sandhanakrishnan, 8, Tarpan, 15

Editorial Credits
Editor: Mandy Robbins; Designer: Dina Her; Media Researcher: Morgan Walters; Production Specialist: Tori Abraham

Printed in the United States of America.
PA117

Table of Contents

Words in **bold** are in the glossary.

Amazing Puffins

What's that black and white bird flying above the sea? It's a puffin! These amazing birds can fly and swim. They spend most of their time at sea. They have colorful **beaks** and markings on their faces. Some people call them "sea parrots."

Puffins are a type of bird. Experts don't agree on how many kinds there are. Some birds are a lot like puffins.

Where in the World

Some puffins live in the northern Atlantic Ocean. They are found from the eastern coast of North America to the coast of Europe. More than half of the world's puffins live near Iceland.

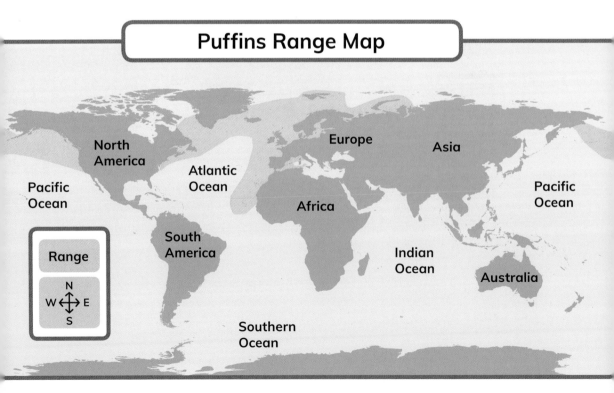

Puffins Range Map

North America

Europe

Asia

Pacific Ocean

Atlantic Ocean

Pacific Ocean

Africa

Range

South America

Indian Ocean

N
W E
S

Australia

Southern Ocean

Other puffins live in the Pacific Ocean. They are found from the coast of Alaska down to California.

Puffins spend most of the year on
the ocean. In the winter, they stay far
away from icy shores. They float on
the water when they aren't flying.

In the summer, they come on land. They stay near the shore. Some live on rocky cliffs. They live in **burrows**. They build nests in the burrow with grass and feathers. This is where they have their young.

Puffin Bodies

Puffins have white and black feathers. The feathers are waterproof. They keep the birds warm and dry in cold ocean water.

Puffins have triangle-shaped beaks. They are very colorful. In the spring, they can turn bright orange, yellow, and red. The bright colors help puffins find a **mate**. In the winter, their colorful beaks fall off. They are left with a smaller gray bill.

Puffins are small birds. They are about 10 inches (25 centimeters) tall. That's shorter than a piece of notebook paper. They weigh around 1 pound (0.5 kilograms). Males are a little bigger than females.

Puffins have short legs. They waddle when they walk. They have sharp claws on their feet. They use their claws and beaks to dig burrows.

Puffins have webbed feet and wings. The webbing helps them swim underwater. They flap their wings to push them through the water. They use their feet to **steer**.

Puffins can also fly. They have short wings. They need a running start to take off. They flap their wings very fast. They can flap them up to 400 times a minute!

On the Menu

A puffin dives into the water. It looks for food. It spots a group of fish. It opens its beak and speeds ahead. Snatch! It has caught its dinner.

Puffins eat small fish. They eat herring and sand eels. They stay underwater for about 30 seconds at a time. They can dive as deep as 200 feet (61 meters).

Puffins can carry a lot of fish in their mouths. They have rough tongues. Their tongues hold fish while they open their beaks to catch more. They catch about 10 fish at once. But they can hold a lot more than that. One puffin was seen with more than 60 fish in its mouth!

Life of a Puffin

Puffins live in groups called **colonies**. Some groups have millions of birds.

Puffins have ways to **communicate**. When a new bird joins a group, it spreads its wings wide open. It puts one foot in front of the other. This tells the others it is friendly.

When puffins are scared or upset, they try to look big. They spread their wings. They open their beaks. They stomp their feet.

Puffins mate in spring and summer. They make nests on land. Male and females usually mate for life. They stay together through summer. Then they leave for the open ocean. They come back to the same burrow every year.

Females usually lay one egg.

Both parents help to keep it warm.

It hatches after about 40 days.

A baby puffin is called a puffling.

Both parents care for the baby puffin. They take turns bringing it food. They guard the burrow.

Babies must stay clean. If they get dirty, they can ruin their waterproof feathers. They use a separate area to go to the bathroom.

Young puffins stay in the burrow up to eight weeks. Then they fly out to sea. They won't return to land for about 3 years. They can live about 20 years in the wild.

Dangers to Puffins

Birds called gulls are a puffin's biggest **predators**. Great black-backed gulls catch puffins in the air. They also swoop down to catch them on land. Other kinds of gulls try to snatch their eggs or babies.

    People threaten puffins too.
In Iceland, they hunt them. People
are also overfishing. That means
puffins may not have enough to eat.
People also dump trash and spill oil
in the ocean. These actions make the
oceans dirty. They can harm puffins.

The number of puffins is going down. But people are trying to help. They are working to protect their nesting spots. Researchers visit them too. They are learning more about them. They are finding ways to save puffins.

Fast Facts

Name: puffin

Habitat: ocean, coasts

Where in the World: Atlantic and Pacific Oceans

Food: small fish, such as herring and sand eels

Predators: gulls, humans

Life span: about 20 years

Glossary

beak (BEEK)—the hard front part of the mouth of birds; also callled a bill

burrow (BUHR-oh)—a hole in the ground that an animal makes

colony (KAH-luh-nee)—a large group of puffins that live together

communicate (kuh-MYOO-nuh-kate)—to share information

mate (MATE)—to join together to produce young

predator (PRED-uh-tur)—an animal that hunts other animals for food

steer (STEER)—to move in a certain direction

Read More

Gibbons, Gail. *The Puffins Are Back!* New York: Holiday House, 2019.

Myers, Maya. *National Geographic Readers: Puffins.* Washington, D.C.: National Geographic Kids, 2019.

Ringstad, Arnold. *Puffins and Penguins.* Mankato, MN: The Child's World, 2020.

Internet Sites

Atlantic Puffin
animalfactguide.com/animal-facts/atlantic-puffin/

Puffin Facts!
www.natgeokids.com/nz/discover/animals/birds/puffin-facts/

Puffins
www.activityvillage.co.uk/puffins

Index